MACMILLAN
BEGINNER LEVEL

ALEXANDRE DUMAS

The Black Tulip

Retold by Florence Bell

MACMILLAN

BEGINNER LEVEL

Founding Editor: John Milne

The Macmillan Readers provide a choice of enjoyable reading materials for learners of English. The series is published at six levels – Starter, Beginner, Elementary, Pre-intermediate, Intermediate and Upper.

Level control
Information, structure and vocabulary are controlled to suit the students' ability at each level.

The number of words at each level:

Starter	about 300 basic words
Beginner	about 600 basic words
Elementary	about 1100 basic words
Pre-intermediate	about 1400 basic words
Intermediate	about 1600 basic words
Upper	about 2200 basic words

Vocabulary
Some difficult words and phrases in this book are important for understanding the story. Some of these words are explained in the story and some are shown in the pictures. From Pre-intermediate level upwards, words are marked with a number like this: ...³. These words are explained in the Glossary at the end of the book.

Contents

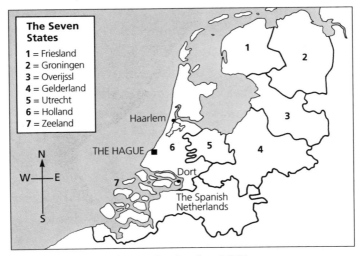

The Netherlands, 1671

A Note About the Author

Alexandre Dumas was French. He was born on 24th July 1802 in Villers-Cotterêts, in northern France. His father was an important soldier – a general in Napoleon's army. Dumas' mother was the daughter of an innkeeper.

In 1823, Dumas went to Paris. He wanted to become a lawyer. But he worked in the house of a rich man. Dumas started to write historical plays and novels. They were exciting and they were successful. Dumas became a famous man. He was one of the most popular French writers of the nineteenth century.

Dumas liked good food, fine wines and beautiful women. He spent a lot of money. He travelled to many countries. He gave money to his friends. Later, he owed money to many people. Then he had to write more books. He had to get more money.

Alexandre Dumas' most famous stories are: *The Three Musketeers* (1844), *Twenty Years After* (1845), *The Count of Monte Cristo* (1844–1845), *The Viscount of Bragelonne* (1844–1850) and *The Black Tulip* (1850).

Dumas died on 5th December 1870 at Puys, near Dieppe, in northern France. He was 68 years old.

A Note About This Story

Time: 1671 to 1673. **Place:** The Netherlands.

In the middle of the nineteenth century, Alexandre Dumas heard two interesting stories about the Netherlands. They were stories about the Netherlands in the seventeenth century. Then Dumas himself wrote a novel about the Netherlands in the 1670s. He put the two interesting stories into his new novel.

One of these stories was about two brothers, John and Cornelius De Witt. The brothers lived in The Hague in the seventeenth century. They were officials in the government of the Dutch Republic.

At that time, the Netherlands belonged to two countries. The area in the south had belonged to Spain for many years. This was the Spanish Netherlands. But France wanted this land, and in 1668, France took a large part of the land. Today, most of this area is called Belgium. The area in the north was the Dutch Republic. Seven states were joined in this republic. These states were Holland, Zeeland, Utrecht, Gelderland, Friesland, Groningen and Overijssl. The Dutch Republic was often called the Seven States. Today, this area is sometimes called Holland and it is sometimes called the Netherlands. The Hague was the capital city of the Seven States.

In the 1670s, there was trouble in the Seven States. Many people wanted a new ruler. Earlier, the ruler of the Seven States had been the Stadtholder. But there had not been a Stadtholder for some years. In the 1670s, some people wanted a new Stadtholder. They wanted William, Prince of Orange. But other people did not want a Stadtholder – they wanted a king. They wanted King Louis XIV of France.

John and Cornelius De Witt did not want a new Stadtholder. They were against the Prince of Orange. But most of the people wanted a new government. They put the De Witts in prison. On 27th August 1672, a crowd of angry people murdered the brothers. And in 1672, William, Prince of Orange, became Stadtholder of the Dutch Republic.

From 1672 to 1678, the Republic was at war with France and England. The French army fought the Dutch army. There were battles on land and in ships at sea. In 1677, William of Orange married an English princess. In 1689, William became King of England, Scotland and Ireland and he moved to Britain.

In the seventeenth century, many people in the Netherlands grew tulips. The first tulips were brought to the Netherlands from Turkey in 1571. Soon, everybody in the Netherlands loved the flowers. Everybody wanted tulips. Stories, songs and poems were written about tulips.

The land in the Netherlands is good. Tulips grow well there. From the seventeenth century, thousands of Dutch people grew tulips. They grew tulips in the ground, in the spring. In the summer, they took the tulip bulbs out of the ground. They put the bulbs in drying-rooms. Then, the people planted their bulbs in the ground in the winter. The flowers grew again in the spring.

Tulip flowers are many different colours. In the seventeenth century, many people tried to grow black tulips. There was going to be a big prize for the grower of the first black tulip.

In the 1840s, Dumas read about the De Witts. And he heard stories about tulips in the Netherlands. Then he wrote a romantic adventure story. He called the story, *The Black Tulip*.

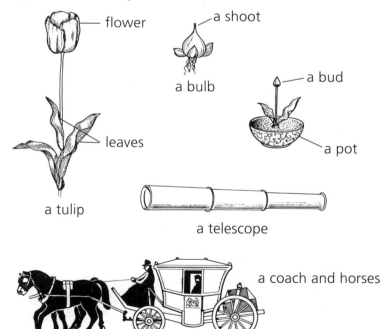

flower

a shoot

a bulb

a bud

leaves

a pot

a tulip

a telescope

a coach and horses

Note: Master = Mr

The People in This Story

Cornelius Van Baerle
kɔːˈneɪlɪjəs fɒn ˈbɑːlə

Isaac Boxtel
ˈaɪzæk ˈbɒkstəl

Cornelius De Witt
kɔːˈneɪlɪjəs də vɪt

John De Witt
dʒɒn də vɪt

Gryphus
ˈgrɪfəs

Rosa
ˈrəʊsə

Craeke
ˈkreɪkə

William, Prince of Orange
ˈwɪljəm, prɪns əv ˈɒrɪndʒ

Van Systens
fɒn ˈsɪstəns

8

Two Tulip-growers

Notice

TO ALL TULIP-GROWERS

GROW A BLACK TULIP

WIN A BIG PRIZE
Win 100 000 guilders

Van Systens
President of the Flower Society
Haarlem

It was November 1671. Men in all the towns in the Seven States were reading this notice. Two of these men lived in the town of Dort. Their names were Isaac Boxtel and Cornelius Van Baerle.

Cornelius Van Baerle was a young man. He was twenty-five years old. He very clever and he was very rich. He loved flowers. And he loved tulips more than all the other flowers. He grew beautiful tulips.

Cornelius Van Baerle was rich but he worked very

hard. He built a special room with very big windows. This was his drying-room. Cornelius grew tulips in his garden. In the summer, he kept the tulip bulbs in his drying-room. In this special room, there were many drawers and cupboards.

'Can I grow a black tulip?' Cornelius asked himself. 'Yes! I have grown dark-blue tulips. I have grown dark-red tulips. Now I will grow a black tulip! It will be very difficult. But I will win the prize.'

'Yes, I will win 100 000 guilders,' Cornelius said to himself. 'But I don't want all the prize money. I will give 50 000 guilders to the poor people of Dort. Then I will travel. I will look for more tulips.'

Cornelius Van Baerle and Isaac Boxtel were neighbours. But they were not friends. Isaac was jealous of Cornelius.

'I hate Cornelius Van Baerle,' Isaac said to himself. 'Why does he grow tulips? He is a scientist. He is very rich. He doesn't want more money!'

Isaac Boxtel was an old man. He had a thin face and white hair. He was the best tulip-grower in Dort. He had been a tulip-grower for many years. He had grown many beautiful tulips.

'I have never seen a black tulip,' Isaac said to himself. 'But I will try to win this prize. I will try to grow a black tulip. I am a poor man. I want to win 100 000 guilders!'

'Cornelius Van Baerle has grown many beautiful tulips,' Isaac thought. 'But he has never grown a black tulip! I will grow a black tulip and I will win the prize. Then I will be rich too.'

———

Every day, Isaac Boxtel saw Cornelius working in his garden. One day, Isaac bought a telescope. After that, he could watch Cornelius in his drying-room too.

In that winter of 1671, Cornelius Van Baerle was working very hard. He was trying to grow a black tulip!

2

The Package

One day, Cornelius Van Baerle had a visitor – a man. The man's name was Cornelius De Witt. Cornelius De Witt was a very important man. He was an official of the government of the Seven States.

Cornelius' brother, John De Witt, was an important man too. He was the leader of the government of the Seven States.

The De Witt brothers lived in The Hague – the capital city of the Seven States. But Cornelius De Witt owned a house in Dort too. And Cornelius De Witt was Cornelius Van Baerle's guardian. The young man's father was dead.

The two men met one evening in January 1672. They met at Cornelius Van Baerle's house in Dort. Cornelius De Witt talked about politics. He talked about his brother, John – the leader of the government of the Seven States.

'I am sorry, sir,' young Cornelius said. 'I am not interested in politics. I am interested in tulips. Please, come to my drying-room. I will show you my bulbs.'

Isaac Boxtel was watching Van Baerle's house through his telescope. He saw some lights in Cornelius' drying-room – the lights from candles. Then Isaac saw the two men in the drying-room. He saw them, but he could not hear them speaking.

Isaac saw Cornelius De Witt give a package to the young man.

Young Cornelius did not open the package. He put it carefully in a drawer. Soon, the two men left the room.

'There are secrets in that package,' Isaac said to himself. 'One day, those secrets will bring trouble to Cornelius Van Baerle.'

The next day, Cornelius De Witt returned to The Hague. And young Cornelius Van Baerle soon forgot about the package. Young Cornelius was not interested in the package. He was interested in his tulips.

———

For many months, Cornelius Van Baerle worked hard. In August, he had a large, special bulb. There were three small bulbs growing out of it.

The young man looked at the special bulb.

'These small bulbs will grow into black tulips. I am sure about that,' he said to himself.

He took the bulb to his drying-room. Carefully, he pulled the three small bulbs from the large bulb.

'Next spring, I will have a black tulip,' he thought. 'Today is the 20th August 1672. In November, I will plant these three small bulbs in the ground. Then, at the end of April 1673, I will have a black tulip!'

3

The Hague Prison

Young Cornelius was happy in Dort. He was very happy about his tulips. But in The Hague, terrible things were happening.

Suddenly, the people of the Seven States wanted to change their government. They did not want John De Witt. They wanted a new leader. Soon, the people hated John De Witt and they hated Cornelius, his brother, too.

'The De Witt brothers are friends of the French king!' the people shouted. 'France is our enemy! We hate the De Witts. We want a new leader. We want Prince William. He is young. He is strong. He must become our leader. Then the Seven States will be strong too!'

In The Hague, people told many strange stories. Nobody knew the truth.

'Cornelius De Witt wants to kill Prince William!' the people said. 'Take Cornelius to the Hague Prison! Punish him! Torture him! Find out about his plans. Then send him away from the Seven States!'

So Cornelius De Witt was taken to the prison in The Hague. There, soldiers tortured him. Cornelius was a good man and he was a brave man. The soldiers injured him badly. The pain was terrible. But he did not tell the soldiers about his plans.

At last, the soldiers took Cornelius to a courtroom. A judge spoke to him.

Cornelius De Witt, you and your brother, John, are bad men. Both of you must leave the Seven States.

The next day, John De Witt and his servant Craeke went to the Hague Prison. They were going to take Cornelius from the prison. Then the three men were going to leave the country.

The jailer of the prison was called Gryphus. He was a bad-tempered old man. Gryphus had a beautiful daughter. She was seventeen years old, and she helped her father at the prison.

'Good morning, Gryphus,' John De Witt said to the old jailer. 'Look, here is a paper from the judges. My brother is not a prisoner now. I am going to take him away from the prison today.'

Gryphus and his daughter took John De Witt to his

brother's cell. Gryphus unlocked the door. Then he walked away.

John De Witt looked at Gryphus' beautiful daughter and he smiled at her.

'What is your name, my dear?' John De Witt asked the girl.

'My name is Rosa, sir,' the girl replied.

'How is my dear brother today, Rosa?' John asked

'His pain is terrible,' Rosa said sadly. There were tears in her blue eyes.

'These are terrible times, sir,' Rosa said. 'The people of the city want to kill your brother. They want to kill you too.'

'But we love our country,' John De Witt replied. 'We have tried to help the people of the Seven States.'

'I know that, sir,' Rosa replied. 'Now, you and your brother must leave the prison quickly. There are many people outside the big gate. They are waiting for you. You and your brother must leave by the small gate. Please tell your brother about my plan.'

John De Witt went into his brother's cell. Cornelius was lying on a bed in the small room.

'My dear Cornelius,' John said. 'We are going to leave the country today. We are in great danger here. Can you walk?'

At that moment, the brothers heard angry shouts. Many people were near the big gate of the prison.

'Give us the De Witt brothers!' the people shouted. 'Bring the traitors out to us.'

'Why do they call us traitors?' John De Witt asked sadly. 'We wanted peace for our country. I wrote letters to the French king. I asked for peace. And King Louis wrote to me. You had those letters, Cornelius. Did you burn them?'

'No, I did not burn the letters,' Cornelius replied. 'One day, those letters will help you, brother. I took those letters to Dort. I gave them to Cornelius Van Baerle.'

'But why did you tell Cornelius about the letters?' John De Witt asked. 'He is not interested in politics.'

'I didn't tell him about the letters,' his brother replied. 'I put those letters in a package. Cornelius Van Baerle did not open the package. He will not open it. He is interested in tulips, not in letters!'

'Then we can save him and we can save ourselves,' John De Witt said. 'Young Cornelius must burn that package. Tell him that. Write to him immediately. I will send Craeke to Dort. He must take your message to young Cornelius today.'

'Yes, I will write to him,' Cornelius De Witt said. 'But I cannot write now. There is no paper here.'

Then Cornelius saw a book next to his bed. He tore a page of white paper from the front of the book.

'I will write on this,' he said.

Quickly, Cornelius wrote a short letter.

> 20 th August 1672
>
> My dear young friend,
> I left a package at your house.
> Please burn the package immediately.
> Do not open it.
>   Your guardian,
>   Cornelius De Witt

John De Witt's servant, Craeke, was waiting outside the cell. John called him.

'Craeke, please take this letter to Dort,' John De Witt said. 'Give it to young Cornelius Van Baerle. He must read the letter immediately. Go quickly!'

Craeke quickly left the cell. Then John spoke to his brother.

'We must go, brother,' he said.

At that moment, Rosa ran into the cell.

'You must go quickly, sirs,' she said. 'Your coach and horses are waiting near the small gate.'

'Thank you, my dear,' Cornelius said. 'You have been very kind to me. I have no money for you. The soldiers took my money. Please take this book. It is yours now.'

'Thank you, sir,' Rosa replied. 'I cannot read. But I will always keep your book. Now, follow me.'

Rosa and the two men left the cell.

4

Murder in the Street

Rosa and the De Witt brothers went out into the prison yard. Rosa unlocked a small gate with a key. A coach and horses were in the street outside the gate.

Get into the coach quickly, sirs!

Drive to the Harbour Gate!

Goodbye, dear Rosa.

The horses pulled the coach away from the prison. Rosa watched it going quickly along the street. Then she ran back into the prison yard and she locked the small gate.

Inside the prison, Rosa met her father.

'The people are outside the big gate. Shall I open it?' the old jailer asked his daughter.

'No, father,' Rosa replied. 'The people will soon break down the big gate. We are in great danger.'

'What will happen to Cornelius De Witt?' Gryphus asked his daughter.

'God will help him and his brother,' Rosa replied.

The angry people soon broke down the big gate. They ran into the prison.

They shouted, 'Death to the traitors! Kill John and Cornelius De Witt!'

———

A young man was standing in a street near the prison. He had a pale face and he was wearing a large hat. The hat nearly covered his eyes. A soldier was standing with him.

The people hate the De Witt brothers. And the people will kill them.

23

The young man smiled but he did not answer.

The De Witts' coach drove up to the Harbour Gate.

The coach driver turned the coach. He started to drive the horses along the narrow street. But some angry people were running towards the gate. They had seen the coach.

'Stop! Stop!' they shouted.

Then suddenly, there were hundreds of angry people in the narrow street. John De Witt looked out of the window of the coach. The people saw his face.

'The traitors!' the people shouted. 'There are the traitors!'

The people ran towards the coach. They stopped the horses. The angry people opened the door of the coach and they pulled out the brothers. The people shouted and screamed. They hit and kicked John and Cornelius De Witt. Soon, the brothers were covered with blood.

The pale young man and the soldier walked towards the coach.

'The people are murdering the De Witt brothers!' the soldier said. 'Sir, we must stop this.'

'We cannot stop it,' the young man said. 'Look! The brothers are dead. The people have killed them. We cannot do anything now.'

The pale young man was William, the Prince of Orange.

'What will the King of France say?' Prince William said to the soldier. 'His dear friends are dead!'

5

The Young Tulip-grower

In Dort, young Cornelius Van Baerle was standing in his drying-room. He was looking at three small tulip bulbs.

'Yes,' he said to himself. 'Next year, these bulbs will be black tulips. I am the happiest man in the Seven States!'

At that moment, a servant ran into the room.

'Somebody wants to see you, sir,' he said. 'He has come from The Hague. His name is Craeke.'

'Craeke?' Cornelius said. 'Craeke is John De Witt's servant. He must wait for a few minutes. I must put these bulbs safely in a drawer.'

'I cannot wait!' a voice shouted. Craeke ran into the room. He was holding a letter in his hand.

Cornelius was very surprised. He dropped the tulip bulbs. They fell onto the floor.

'Please, read this letter!' Craeke said. 'Please read it immediately, sir.'

'I will read the letter,' Cornelius said. 'But I must pick up my bulbs first.'

He picked up the tulip bulbs and he looked at them carefully.

'Good,' he said quietly. 'The bulbs are not damaged. I thank God for that.'

But Craeke had put the letter on a table and he had

left the house.

Suddenly, one of Cornelius' servants ran into the drying room.

'Oh, sir!' the servant said. 'There are soldiers in the house. They are going to arrest you, sir!'

'They are going to arrest me? I do not understand,' Cornelius said.

Cornelius was not frightened. He was thinking of his black tulip bulbs. He picked up Craeke's letter from the table. He did not read it. The letter was written on a piece of white paper – a white page from a book. Very carefully, Cornelius put the paper round the three tulip bulbs – he made a package. Then he put the little package into his pocket.

Four soldiers ran into the room. A judge was with them. The judge was from the courtroom in Dort. The judge had received a message from Isaac Boxtel.

'Cornelius Van Baerle, you have some papers,' the judge said. 'They are the papers of a traitor. Give the papers to me!'

'I don't understand,' Cornelius said.

'Last January, Cornelius De Witt left a package of papers in this house,' the judge said. 'You must give that package to me.'

'No, I cannot give the package to you,' the young man replied. 'It is not mine.'

'I must take those papers!' the judge shouted. He pointed to a large drawer. 'They are in that drawer,' he said.

The judge opened the drawer and took out the package. He opened the package and he looked at the letters inside it.

'Yes! You are a traitor too,' the judge said. 'I arrest you, Cornelius Van Baerle. You are a prisoner now. You must come with me to The Hague.'

Isaac Boxtel was watching Cornelius Van Baerle's house. He was watching through his telescope. He saw the soldiers going into his neighbour's house. And he saw the judge.

'Good! The judge has got my message,' Isaac said to himself. 'But I did not put my name in that message. I am not in danger. The soldiers will take Cornelius Van Baerle to The Hague. They will put him in prison there. Then they will kill him. Good! I will take his tulip bulbs.'

That night, Boxtel went into Cornelius' house. He

went into the house through a window. The house was empty. The servants had run away. Isaac went into the drying-room. He looked for the bulbs of the black tulip.

'The bulbs are here, in this room,' Isaac said to himself. 'Cornelius told his friends about them. He said, "I will have a black tulip next spring." But where are those bulbs?'

Isaac looked in all the drawers and he looked in all the cupboards. There were many bulbs in the drawers and cupboards. And all the bulbs had names. Isaac Boxtel looked at each name. He knew all these names. None of these was a black tulip!

Isaac did not find the bulbs of the black tulip. But he found Cornelius Van Baerle's notebook. Cornelius had written about his tulips in the notebook. On one page, Isaac read these words.

> 20th August 1672
> Today, I have three small tulip bulbs from one large bulb. These bulbs will have flowers in the spring of 1673. The flowers will be black. I thank God.

'Those bulbs! Where are they?' Isaac Boxtel said. 'Oh, I understand now. Cornelius has taken them. He has taken them to The Hague. I must go to The Hague too!'

6

Cornelius and Rosa

Cornelius Van Baerle was sitting in the Hague Prison. He was sitting on a bed in a cell. Two people were looking at him – the jailer, Gryphus, and Rosa, the jailer's beautiful daughter.

'Young man, you are in a your guardian's cell,' the jailer said. He laughed loudly.

'What do you mean?' Cornelius asked him.

'Cornelius De Witt was in this cell,' Gryphus replied. 'His brother, John, was here too. But they are not coming back!'

'Where are they now?' Cornelius asked.

Gryphus laughed again.

'They are both dead,' Gryphus said. 'They were killed by the people.'

'They were kind gentlemen,' Rosa said. 'They were not traitors.'

'They were enemies of Prince William,' Gryphus said to his daughter. 'You are an enemy of Prince William too!' he said to Cornelius.

Rosa looked at the handsome young man. She liked him very much. She started to cry. Cornelius turned away. He was sad.

Gryphus pushed his daughter out of the cell. Then he left the cell and he locked the door.

———

The next day, some soldiers took Cornelius to the courtroom in The Hague. He stood in front of a judge.

'You are a traitor,' the judge said. 'You will die!'

Cornelius was taken back to his cell in the prison. Soon, Rosa came to the cell.

Cornelius put the bulbs back in the paper. Then he gave the package to the young girl.

Next spring, I will be dead. The bulbs are yours now, Rosa. There will be a prize for the first black tulip – 100 000 guilders!

That is a lot of money!

Yes. With that money, you will get married to a fine young man.

I will never get married. You will not be alive.

Suddenly, there was a noise outside the cell.

'The soldiers are coming,' Cornelius said. 'They are going to take me away and they are going to kill me.'

'Take care of the bulbs,' said Cornelius. 'Plant them in the ground in November. Goodbye, dear Rosa.'

The door opened. Soldiers came into the cell. They held Cornelius' arms. They took him out of the prison. They took him to a wide square near the city hall. The city executioner was waiting in the middle of the square. He was holding a huge, sharp sword.

Hundreds of people were standing in the square. All these people wanted to watch Cornelius' execution. The executioner was going to cut off the young man's head. Isaac Boxtel was watching too.

The young man knelt on the ground, in front of the executioner. The executioner lifted his heavy sword.

Then a man ran out of the city hall. He was holding a letter and he was shouting.

'Stop!' the man shouted. 'Cornelius Van Baerle will not die today. Prince William is good to his enemies. But Cornelius Van Baerle is a dangerous man. He will go back to the prison. And he will stay in prison all his life!'

'I thank God,' Cornelius said to himself. 'I will see Rosa again today – and I will see my tulip bulbs!'

But Cornelius was wrong. He did not go back to the Hague Prison. The soldiers took him to the prison at Lovenstein, far away from The Hague.

Cornelius was unhappy. He was far away from his tulip bulbs. He was far away from Rosa.

Isaac Boxtel was unhappy too. And he was very angry. He wanted Cornelius' black tulip.

7

Lovenstein Prison

Time passed. It was November 1672. Cornelius Van Baerle was in a cell in Lovenstein Prison, near Dort. The cell was a small room with stone walls. It had a strong wooden door. There was a small window in the door. And there was a window in the stone wall. From this window, Cornelius could look at the town of Dort. He could look at his own house.

'But I will never live in my house again,' Cornelius said to himself. 'I will never grow a black tulip. I will never see my tulip bulbs again. And I will never see Rosa again. Will she plant the bulbs? Will she grow a black tulip? I will never know.'

But Cornelius was wrong. He did see his tulip bulbs again. And he did see Rosa.

One morning, he heard a girl's voice outside his cell. It was Rosa's voice!

The small window in the cell door opened and the young man saw Rosa's face. It was pale and sad.

'Oh, Rosa, Rosa!' Cornelius said.

'Speak quietly! My father is near,' Rosa said.

'Your father? Why are you both here?' Cornelius asked.

'My father is old,' Rosa replied. 'He wanted to work in a smaller prison. We have come to Lovenstein. My father is the jailer of this prison now. You are here,

Cornelius. You are safe. I thank God for that. Your tulip bulbs are safe too, Cornelius!'

'Oh, Rosa, do you love me?' Cornelius asked.

'Yes!' Rosa replied with a smile. 'I love you very much. I will come back this evening at nine o'clock. Goodbye, Cornelius, my dear.'

Cornelius was a happy man.

'I will never leave this prison,' he said to himself. 'But Rosa will grow my black tulip. Then she will be rich. She will be happy.'

———

That evening, Cornelius waited for Rosa. He heard a bell ringing. He listened. The bell rang nine times. Then the small window in the cell door opened and Cornelius saw Rosa's face again.

'Here I am,' Rosa said. 'Every night, I will give my father some strong wine. He will fall asleep. Then I will come here and talk to you.'

'Look, Cornelius! I have your tulip bulbs here,' she said. 'They are safe in the paper package. Take them. They are yours, they are not mine.'

'No, Rosa,' Cornelius said. 'I have a better idea. I will take one of the bulbs. I will try to grow it. There is a bowl here in my cell.'

'Please bring me some earth tomorrow,' Cornelius said. 'I will plant the bulb in the bowl. You must plant the second bulb in the ground. Take care of it. But keep the third bulb in the paper package.'

'We have a garden here,' Rosa said. 'The earth in the garden is good. I will bring you some earth for your bowl. Each of us will grow a black tulip. God will help us.'

Cornelius and Rosa talked for half an hour. Then Rosa said, 'I must go now. Goodnight, my dear.'

She gave one of the tulip bulbs to Cornelius. But she kept the other two bulbs.

On the next three evenings, Rosa brought the young man some earth from her garden. He put the earth into his bowl. On the third evening, he planted his bulb in the earth.

Rosa planted one of her bulbs too. But she did not plant it in her garden. She planted it in a pot.

And Rosa kept the pot in her own room.

Time passed. Every evening, Rosa's father fell asleep after supper. And every evening, at nine o'clock, Rosa went to Cornelius' cell.

'Oh, Rosa, you are very kind to me,' Cornelius said one evening. 'How can I help you?'

Rosa smiled.

'I cannot read or write. But I want to read and write,' she said. 'Will you be my teacher, Cornelius?'

'I have no books, Rosa,' Cornelius said.

'I have a book,' Rosa replied. 'Cornelius De Witt, your guardian, gave me a book. Please be my teacher, Cornelius.'

Cornelius smiled at Rosa.

'Yes. I will be your teacher,' he said.

8

Jacob Gisels

Slowly, the winter passed. Every evening, Rosa came to Cornelius' cell. Rosa always held a candle. The light from the candle shone on her beautiful face and her golden hair. Every evening, she brought her book with her. She held the book near the window in the cell door. Cornelius taught the girl about reading and about writing. He pointed to the letters and words in the book. He spoke the letters and words. Rosa loved the young man. And Cornelius loved her too. Sometimes, their hands touched through the little window.

But one evening, Rosa was half an hour late.

'Don't be angry with me,' she said to Cornelius. 'My father has a visitor. This man met my father at the Hague Prison. He comes here every day. He buys wine for my father.'

'Does this man ask questions about me?' Cornelius asked Rosa.

Rosa smiled.

'No!' Rosa replied. 'He is not interested in you, Cornelius. He is interested in me!'

'Is this man young?' Cornelius asked. 'Is he a handsome man?'

'No!' Rosa said again. 'He is old and he is very ugly. He has a thin face and white hair. His name is Jacob Gisels.'

———

Old Gryphus came into Cornelius' cell three times every day. He brought food and water for the prisoner. The old jailer was a very bad-tempered man. He always shouted at Cornelius.

Cornelius kept his tulip bowl in a dark corner of his cell. Every day, he looked at it carefully.

One morning, he saw a green shoot. The tulip was growing! Cornelius held the bowl in his hands. He was very happy. He did not hear Gryphus unlocking the cell door.

'What is in the bowl?' Gryphus shouted.

'It is a tulip,' Cornelius replied.

'Why are you growing a tulip?' said Gryphus.

The jailer put his hands on the bowl and he held it. He pulled it. But Cornelius held the bowl too. Gryphus put his fingers into the bowl. He pulled out the tulip bulb. He threw the bulb onto the floor and he put his foot on it!

Cornelius shouted loudly. He lifted the bowl above the jailer's head. He was going to hit the old man with the bowl. But at that moment, he heard Rosa's voice.

'Stop! Stop!' Rosa shouted. She ran into the cell.

'Father, what have you done?' Rosa said.

'I stood on a tulip bulb, that is all,' Gryphus said. 'A tulip bulb is nothing. Come, Rosa, leave the prisoner alone. He is mad!'

Gryphus went back to his room.

But Jacob Gisels had heard the shouts. He went to the jailer's room.

'What is wrong, Master Gryphus?' he asked the old jailer.

'Nothing is wrong, Master Jacob,' Gryphus replied. 'A mad prisoner was shouting. His name is Cornelius Van Baerle. He was shouting about a tulip bulb. That is all. One tulip bulb!'

'A tulip bulb? Where is it? Let me see it!' Jacob shouted.

'I put my foot on it,' Gryphus said. He laughed.

'You old fool!' Jacob shouted. 'Where are the other bulbs?'

'The others? Soon there will be hundreds of tulips in the market,' Gryphus replied. 'Buy some tulips in the market, Jacob.'

At that moment, Rosa came into her father's room.

'That bulb was special,' Rosa said quietly.

Jacob Gisels looked at the young girl carefully.

'What do you know about tulips, Rosa?' he asked.

'I know nothing about tulips,' Rosa replied quickly. 'But the prisoner loved that tulip. My father was unkind.'

———

At nine o'clock that evening, Rosa went to Cornelius' cell. She told Jacob's words to Cornelius.

Cornelius became pale. He was worried.

'This man – Jacob Gisels – wants to steal my tulip bulbs,' he said. 'Take care of the third bulb, Rosa. Please do not come to see me tomorrow. You will be in danger here.'

'I understand, Cornelius,' Rosa said. She began to cry.

'I must take care of the tulip bulbs, but I must not visit you,' Rosa said. 'You love your tulips. But you do not love me. Goodbye, Cornelius.'

Rosa went away quickly. Cornelius sat on his bed in the dark cell. He was very sad.

That night, the young man dreamt many dreams. But he did not dream about black tulips. He dreamt about Rosa's blue eyes. Cornelius loved Rosa very much.

9

The Black Tulip

Rosa was very unhappy. She was alone in her room.

'Cornelius loves his tulips more than me,' she thought.

Rosa looked sadly at a large pot in a corner of her room. Cornelius had said, 'Plant the second bulb in the ground.' But she had not done that. The second bulb was not in the ground. It was in the pot in her room. Rosa had not told Cornelius about the pot.

'Will this bulb grow?' Rosa asked herself. 'Will it become a black tulip?'

Rosa looked at the pot for many hours. But she did not visit Cornelius.

'He doesn't want to see me,' Rosa said to herself.

Every evening, Cornelius waited for Rosa. But she did not come to his cell.

'The young prisoner will soon be dead,' Gryphus said to Rosa one day. 'He won't eat and he won't drink.'

Rosa became pale.

'Cornelius is unhappy about his tulips,' she thought.

The next morning, she pushed a note under the door of Cornelius' cell.

Don't be unhappy, Cornelius. Your tulips are safe.
Rosa

And Cornelius wrote a reply on the back of the paper. He pushed the paper under the door for Rosa.

The tulips are not important. But I want to see you, my dear, dear Rosa. Cornelius

The next evening, Rosa came to Cornelius' cell.

'Oh, my beautiful Rosa,' Cornelius said. 'I have been very unhappy. What is your news?'

'Jacob Gisels went into my garden this morning,'

Rosa replied. 'He was looking for something there.'

'He will find the second tulip!' Cornelius said.

Rosa smiled.

'Your second tulip is safe,' she said. 'I did not plant the bulb in the garden. I planted it in a pot. It is in my room.'

'I thank God for that!' Cornelius said.

Rosa smiled sadly.

'First, you love your black tulip,' she said. 'Then you love me.'

'That is not true, Rosa,' Cornelius replied. 'But you must grow the black tulip. You will win 100000 guilders. Then you will marry a good man. You will leave this terrible place.'

'Do you want me to go?' Rosa asked sadly.

'No, I want to see you every day,' Cornelius replied. 'I love you, Rosa.'

'Then I will come here every day!' Rosa said. 'But do not say the words "black tulip" for three days!'

Rosa smiled at the young man.

'I will never say those words again,' Cornelius replied.

Rosa laughed. She put her face next to the little window in the door. Cornelius touched her face with his lips.

Cornelius was in prison, but he was a happy man. Rosa loved him. And his black tulip was safe in her room.

The next day, Gryphus told his friend, Jacob Gisels,

about the prisoner.

'Cornelius Van Baerle is a happy man today,' the jailer said.

'Why is he happy? Has he hidden something in his cell?' Gisels asked.

'Yes! You are right!' Gryphus said. 'Tomorrow, I will look for it.'

The next day, Gryphus looked everywhere in the prisoner's cell. But he did not find anything. Cornelius laughed at him.

After two more days, Rosa had some good news.

'Your tulip is growing,' she said.

———

After that, Rosa brought news of the tulip every day.

One day, Rosa said, 'And now the bud is...BLACK!'

'The bud is black, Rosa? Are you sure about that?' Cornelius asked.

'Your tulip bud is black, my dear Cornelius,' Rosa replied. 'The flower will be black.'

'It is not my tulip. It is your tulip, Rosa,' Cornelius said. 'Now, listen to me. You must take the tulip to Haarlem.'

'I must take it to Haarlem? No! I will not leave you, Cornelius,' said Rosa.

'Then the President of the Flower Society must come here,' Cornelius said. 'He must come to Lovenstein. He must see our black tulip!'

The next evening, Rosa brought the flower to Cornelius' cell. The tulip was tall and straight. The bud had opened. The flower was beautiful. And it was black!

'I thank God!' Cornelius said. 'God has given us our black tulip. And the tulip is safe!'

But Cornelius was wrong. His beautiful tulip was in great danger!

10

The Truth at Last

Who was Jacob Gisels? Jacob Gisels was Isaac Boxtel!
Why was Isaac Boxtel in Lovenstein? He wanted the
black tulip! He wanted to win 100 000 guilders!

Boxtel watched Rosa every day. He saw her in her
little garden.

But the tulip was not in the garden. Where was it?
He could not find it anywhere. Then, at last, Boxtel
understood. The black tulip was in Rosa's room! It was
growing in a pot!

Boxtel wanted to steal the black tulip. But Rosa

always locked the door of her room. The key was always in her pocket.

So Isaac Boxtel made some new keys. One afternoon, he tried to open Rosa's door with them. At last, one of the keys turned in the lock. Isaac opened the door and he went into Rosa's room.

———

'Cornelius! Cornelius!' Rosa shouted. Her face was very pale. She was crying.

'Rosa! What is wrong?' Cornelius asked. 'Why are you unhappy this evening?'

'The tulip! The black tulip has gone,' Rosa said. 'Somebody has stolen it!'

'Did you lock your door today?' Cornelius asked.

'Yes! I always lock my door,' Rosa replied.

'Jacob Gisels has stolen the tulip, Rosa,' said Cornelius. 'I must get out of this cell. Take the key from your father. I will kill Gryphus and I will kill Gisels! Open this door, please Rosa.'

'Please, be quiet, dear Cornelius,' Rosa said. 'My father will hear you. I will take my father's key now.'

'You will never take my key!' a voice shouted.

It was Gryphus! He was near the cell and he was listening to the two young people.

49

Gryphus hit his daughter and he shouted at her.

'I will tell Prince William about this! And you will never see this prisoner again!' Gryphus shouted.

———

The next morning, Isaac Boxtel and the black tulip were in Haarlem. Boxtel wrote a letter to the President of the Flower Society.

> Dear Sir,
> I have grown a black tulip. I will bring it to your house today. I will win the prize of 100 000 guilders. I am staying at the White Swan Inn.
> Isaac Boxtel

———

Boxtel's plan was clever. But Rosa was clever too and she was brave. And she was in love with Cornelius Van Baerle.

'I must go to Haarlem,' Rosa said to herself. 'I must go there today. I must talk to the President of the Flower Society.'

Rosa put some clothes in a bag. She put the third tulip bulb in her bag too. The bulb was in the package – the paper from Cornelius De Witt's book. A few hours later, Rosa was travelling to Haarlem.

In the afternoon, Gryphus looked for his daughter. And he looked for his friend, Jacob Gisels. Where were they? Had they gone away together?

Gryphus was very angry. He went to Cornelius' cell.

He asked the prisoner about Rosa. He shouted at the young man. He hit the prisoner. But Cornelius did not fight the jailer. His tulip had gone. He did not want to live.

———

Rosa arrived in Haarlem. She was tired, but she went to the house of the President of the Flower Society. Van Systens, the President, talked to her.

'I want to tell you about the black tulip, sir,' Rosa said. 'Somebody has stolen the black tulip from me.'

Van Systens, looked at the beautiful girl. He was very surprised.

'We will soon find the thief,' he said. 'I saw the black tulip two hours ago. Master Isaac Boxtel brought it here. Are you Master Isaac Boxtel's servant?'

'No, sir, I do not know Master Boxtel.' Rosa replied.

'The tulip is mine and it was stolen from me.'

'Are there two black tulips in Haarlem?' the President asked. 'I don't believe it!'

'Is Master Boxtel an old man? Does he have a thin face?' Rosa asked.

'Yes,' the President replied. 'Why are you asking me these questions?'

'Master Boxtel is the thief, sir,' Rosa replied. 'The black tulip is not Master Boxtel's. It is mine.'

'Be very careful, young woman,' the President said. 'Do not call Master Boxtel a thief. You have made a mistake. Visit Master Boxtel now and talk to him. He is staying at the White Swan Inn.'

Rosa left the President's house.

'What shall I do?' she asked herself. 'Is Jacob Gisels Isaac Boxtel? I don't know. But Gisels will never give the black tulip to me.'

Rosa walked slowly through the busy streets of Haarlem. All the people in the streets were talking about the black tulip.

'Have you seen the black tulip?' they asked each other. 'There is a black tulip here, in Haarlem. Somebody has won the prize. Who is it?'

'I will go back to the President,' Rosa said to herself. 'I will tell him my story. He will believe me!'

———

The President was busy. He did not want to see Rosa again. But the beautiful girl ran into his sitting-room. She knelt on the floor by his feet.

'Please go away. I am busy,' the President said. 'I am writing a report about the black tulip.'

'But your report will not be true, sir,' Rosa said. 'Please bring Master Boxtel here. He must bring the black tulip with him. Let me see them.'

At that moment, they heard shouts in the street.

'Wait here for a minute!' the President said. He ran from the room.

A pale young man had come into the house.

'Prince William!' the President said. 'Welcome to Haarlem. Welcome to my house!'

Prince William smiled.

'I want to see the black tulip,' he said. 'Is it here?'

'No, sir,' Van Systens said. 'The black tulip is at the White Swan Inn. The tulip-grower has it. He is Isaac Boxtel of Dort. But there is a problem, sir.'

'A problem?' Prince William asked.

'Yes, sir,' Van Systens replied. 'A young girl came here today. She said, "Isaac Boxtel did not grow the tulip. He stole it. The black tulip is mine." The girl is here now, sir.'

'Is the girl telling the truth?' Prince William asked.

'I don't know, sir,' the President replied.

'You must send a servant for Boxtel,' said the Prince. 'Boxtel must bring the tulip here. Let the girl see the tulip. Then ask Boxtel and the girl questions about it. I will watch and listen.'

Van Systens sent a servant to the White Swan Inn. Then the President started to ask Rosa questions. Prince William listened.

'Are you the grower of the tulip?' he asked.

'Yes, sir,' Rosa said. 'I grew it in my room. I am the daughter of the jailer of Lovenstein Prison.'

'Do you know about tulips?' the President asked.

'No, sir,' Rosa replied. 'A prisoner in Lovenstein gave me the bulb. I grew the tulip for him.'

Then Rosa told Van Systens her story. She told him about her first meeting with Cornelius. She told him about her love for Cornelius. And she told him about the young man's love for her. Prince William listened.

'Was this prisoner in the Hague Prison too?' the Prince asked.

'Yes, sir,' Rosa replied.

'He is a lucky prisoner!' Prince William said. And he smiled.

11

The Letter

'Master Boxtel has arrived, sir,' Van Systens said to
Prince William. The Prince sat in a corner of the
room.

Isaac Boxtel came into the room. He put the black
tulip on a table.

'That is my tulip!' Rosa said. 'And this man was at
Lovenstein Prison. He called himself Jacob Gisels. He
bought wine for my father. And he took the tulip from
my room in the prison.'

Isaac Boxtel looked at Rosa. Then Boxtel saw
Prince William. Suddenly, Boxtel was very frightened.

'Prince William!' he said. 'I did not steal this tulip. I am Isaac Boxtel. Everybody in Dort knows me. I have grown tulips in Dort for twenty years. This girl and her friend tried to steal my tulip.'

'Her friend?' Prince William asked. 'Who is her friend?'

'He is a prisoner in Lovenstein prison,' Boxtel said. 'His name is Cornelius Van Baerle. He was a friend of the traitor, Cornelius De Witt. The prisoner is a traitor too. And he is a thief!'

Rosa started to cry. She turned to Prince William.

'Oh, sir! That is not true,' the young girl said. 'This man is telling lies. Cornelius is not a thief and he is not a traitor.'

'I will not punish you, young woman,' Prince William said. 'But I punish thieves and traitors.'

'Sir, let me ask Master Boxtel some questions,' Rosa said.

'I will answer your questions,' Boxtel said.

'Is this your tulip?' Rosa asked.

'Yes, it is,' Boxtel replied.

'How many small bulbs were there on the large bulb?'

'Two – no – three. There were three,' Boxtel replied.

'And what happened to the other bulbs?' Rosa asked.

'One bulb did not grow,' Boxtel replied. 'But the second bulb grew into this tulip.'

'And the third?' Rosa asked quietly.

'It is in my house, in Dort,' said Boxtel.

'That is not true,' Rosa said. 'I have the third bulb here. Cornelius Van Baerle gave it to me, last year. It is in this paper package. Look!'

Then Rosa took the third bulb from the paper – the paper from Cornelius De Witt's book. She showed the bulb to Van Systens and the Prince. Suddenly, she looked at the piece of paper. There was some writing on the paper. And Rosa could read it! Cornelius had taught her about reading. Rosa read the writing for the first time. Then she smiled.

'Read this! Read this, sir!' Rosa said. She gave the paper to Prince William.

The Prince read the writing quietly.

20 th August 1672

My dear young friend,
I left a package at your house.
Please burn the package immediately.
Do not open it.
Your guardian,
Cornelius De Witt

Prince William smiled. He put the paper in his pocket.

'There is a prize for the first black tulip,' he said. 'I will be the judge for the black tulip prize. Master Van Systens, please take care of this girl and the tulip. Goodbye, Master Boxtel. I will see you again.'

Boxtel walked slowly out of the room. He did not understand the Prince's words.

Rosa went close to the black tulip and she kissed it. Then she spoke to Prince William.

'Prince William,' she said. 'Cornelius Van Baerle taught me about reading. I thank God for that. Sir, you know the truth. Please help me. Please help my dear Cornelius!'

12

The Prize

Cornelius was standing in his prison cell. Gryphus was in the cell too. He was shouting at Cornelius.

'Where is my daughter?' the old jailer shouted.

Gryphus had been drinking wine. And he was holding a heavy stick.

'Where is Rosa?' Gryphus asked again. 'I will hit you with this stick. And then you will tell me the truth!'

Gryphus lifted his stick and he hit Cornelius. But Cornelius was stronger than the old jailer. He took the stick and he hit the old man.

'Help! Help!' Gryphus shouted 'The prisoner is killing me! Help! Help!'

Some soldiers ran into the cell. They took the stick from Cornelius. Then they left the cell. The old jailer went with them. He locked the door.

'I hit the jailer,' Cornelius said to himself, sadly. 'Now I will die and I will never see Rosa again.'

Two hours passed. Then the cell door opened again. Four soldiers ran into the cell.

'Cornelius Van Baerle, you must come with us!' one of them said.

The soldiers took Cornelius out of the prison. They put him in a coach. Quickly, the horses pulled the coach towards Haarlem.

In Haarlem, the people were very happy. Somebody had grown a black tulip. And Prince William was in Haarlem. The Prince was going to give the prize.

The President of the Flower Society carried the black tulip through the city. Everybody shouted. Prince William rode on a black horse. He rode behind Van Systens. They went towards the wide square in front of the city hall. Many thousands of people were standing in the square.

Cornelius Van Baerle was in Haarlem too. The soldiers had brought him there in the coach. The coach had stopped in the wide square. Cornelius looked out of the window of the coach.

'Why are all these people here?' Cornelius asked a man. 'Are they going to watch my execution?'

'No, no!' the man shouted. 'Somebody has grown a black tulip. Prince William is going to give the prize!'

'A black tulip? Where is it?' Cornelius shouted.

Prince William was near the coach, and he heard Cornelius' words. He stopped his horse.

'Who is this man?' Prince William asked one of the soldiers.

'This is the prisoner from Lovenstein,' the soldier said. 'You wanted him here, in Haarlem, sir.'

'Let this man see the black tulip,' said the Prince.

Then he rode towards the city hall.

A few minutes later, the soldiers took Cornelius out of the coach. They walked slowly to the city hall. Prince William was sitting on a big chair in front of the city hall. And next to the Prince's chair was a table. On the table was the black tulip. Suddenly, the people were quiet.

Isaac Boxtel became pale. He looked at Rosa.

Isaac looked at Cornelius.

Prince William spoke to Rosa and Cornelius.

'You are both the growers of the black tulip,' the Prince said. 'This beautiful flower will be called "Rosa Van Baerle". Cornelius Van Baerle, here is your wife. You are free. Rosa, here is your husband. You have both won the prize of 100 000 guilders!'

Then Prince William took something from his pocket. It was Cornelius De Witt's letter.

'I have read this letter and now I know the truth,' Prince William said to the people. 'Cornelius Van Baerle is not a traitor. The people of The Hague killed John and Cornelius De Witt. But the people did a bad thing! The De Witt brothers were not traitors. They were both good men. They loved their country.'

———

A few days later, Cornelius and Rosa got married. Soon, they had two beautiful children. And they grew many more beautiful tulips.

63

Published by Macmillan Heinemann ELT
Between Towns Road, Oxford OX4 3PP
Macmillan Heinemann ELT is an imprint of
Macmillan Publishers Limited
Companies and representatives throughout the world
Heinemann is a registered trademark of Harcourt Education, used under licence.

ISBN 978-1-4050-7228-1

This retold version by Florence Bell for Macmillan Readers
First published 1998
Text © Florence Bell 1998, 2002, 2005
Design and illustration © Macmillan Publishers Limited 1998, 2002, 2005

This edition first published 2005

Illustrated by Gerry Ball
Original cover template design by Jackie Hill
Cover photography by Alamy
Acknowledgements: The publishers would like to thank Popperfoto for
permission to reproduce the picture on page 4.

Printed in Thailand

2011   2010   2009   2008   2007
9   8   7   6   5   4   3